MAD FOR MADHU
- VOLUME ONE | EDITION ONE-

A Colouring Book for Adults

The illustrations in this colouring book

were developed at

Studio 324

by our resident artist

Shikha Banerjee.

Content written and edited by:

Studio 324

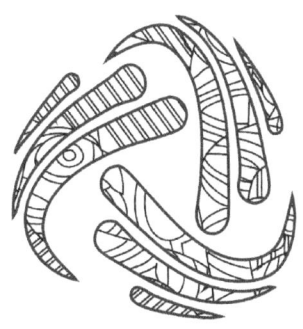

ISBN
978-0-9952904-0-2

Published by
Studio 324
Printed by CreateSpace
Charleston, SC

Eye-catching geometric patterns made using natural dyes and pigments with fingers, twigs, brushes, nib-pens, and matchsticks characterise the traditional art form called **MADHUBANI** from the Indian sub-continent.

MADHUBANI
patterns vary from mildly simple to wildly intricate! We've developed illustrations that range from

EASY to MEDIUM to TOUGH

As the pages turn, you'll see the patterns get more intricate and your attention to detail more keen.
We've progressively increased the complexity to provide a range for our colourists. As you go through the book, you'll see yourself developing a stronger control over your colouring skills as well as understand what shades complement each other best.

STUDIO 324
brings to you this colouring book that captures the essence of this art form.

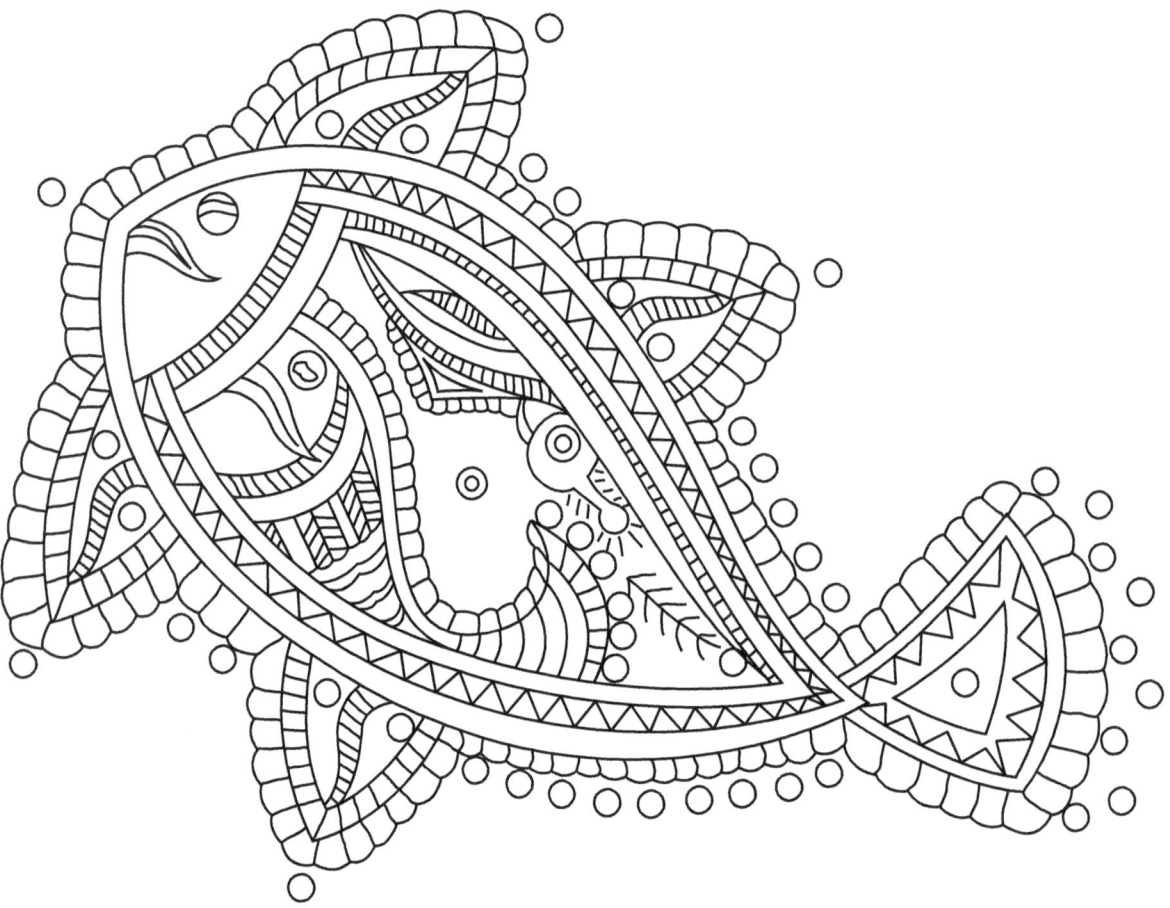

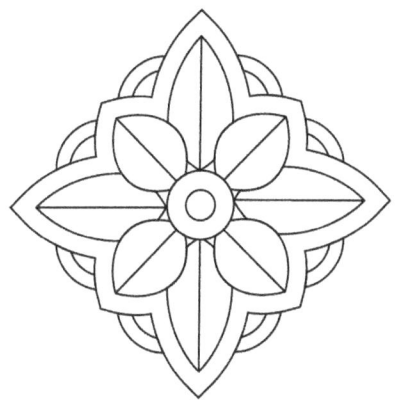

This book belongs to

_____

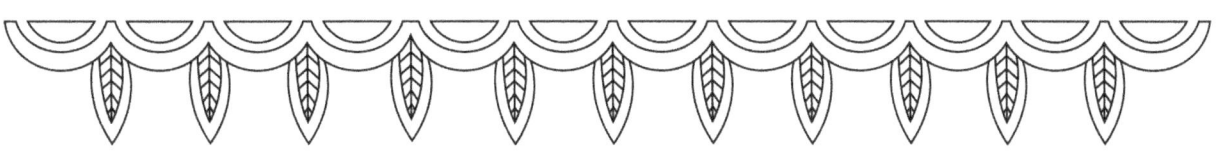

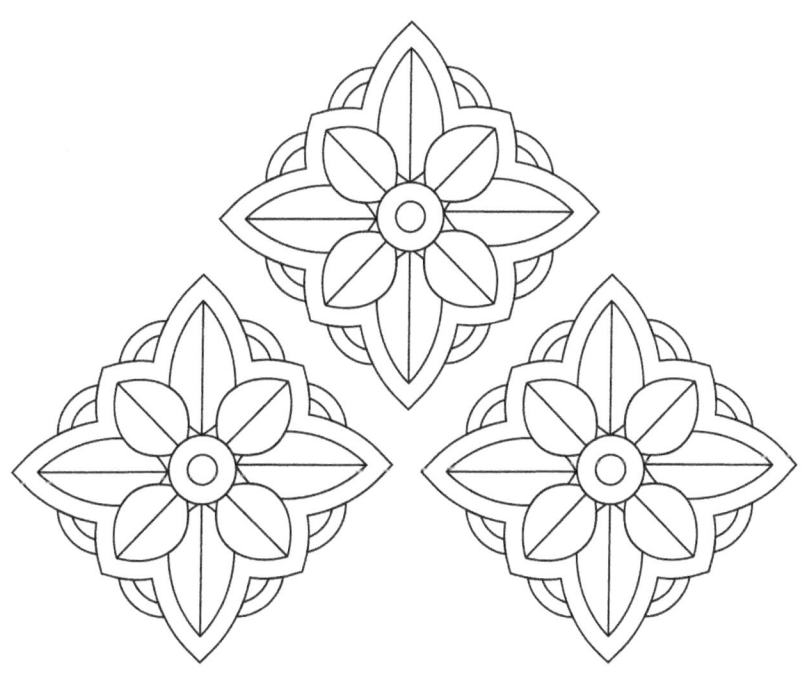

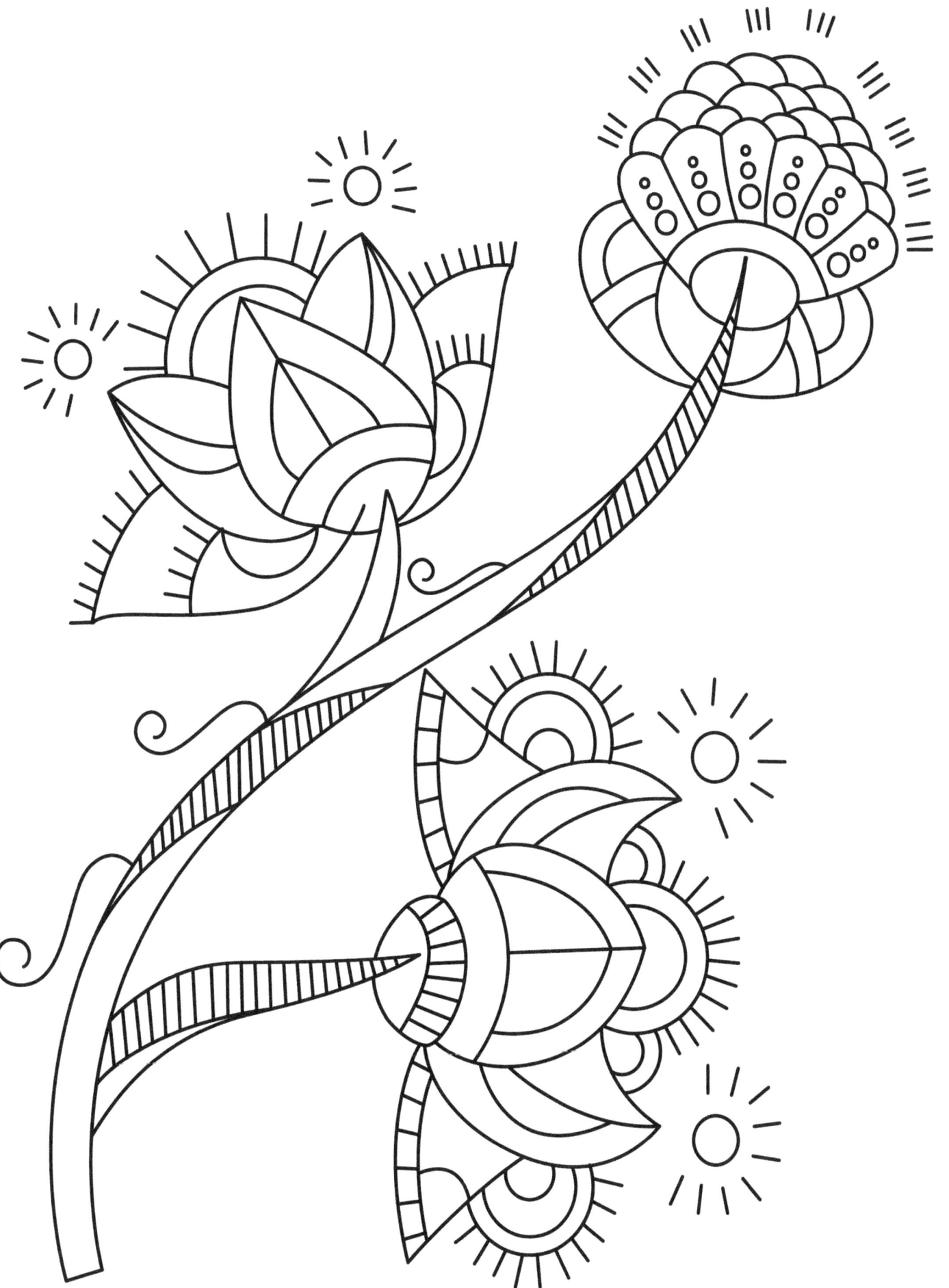

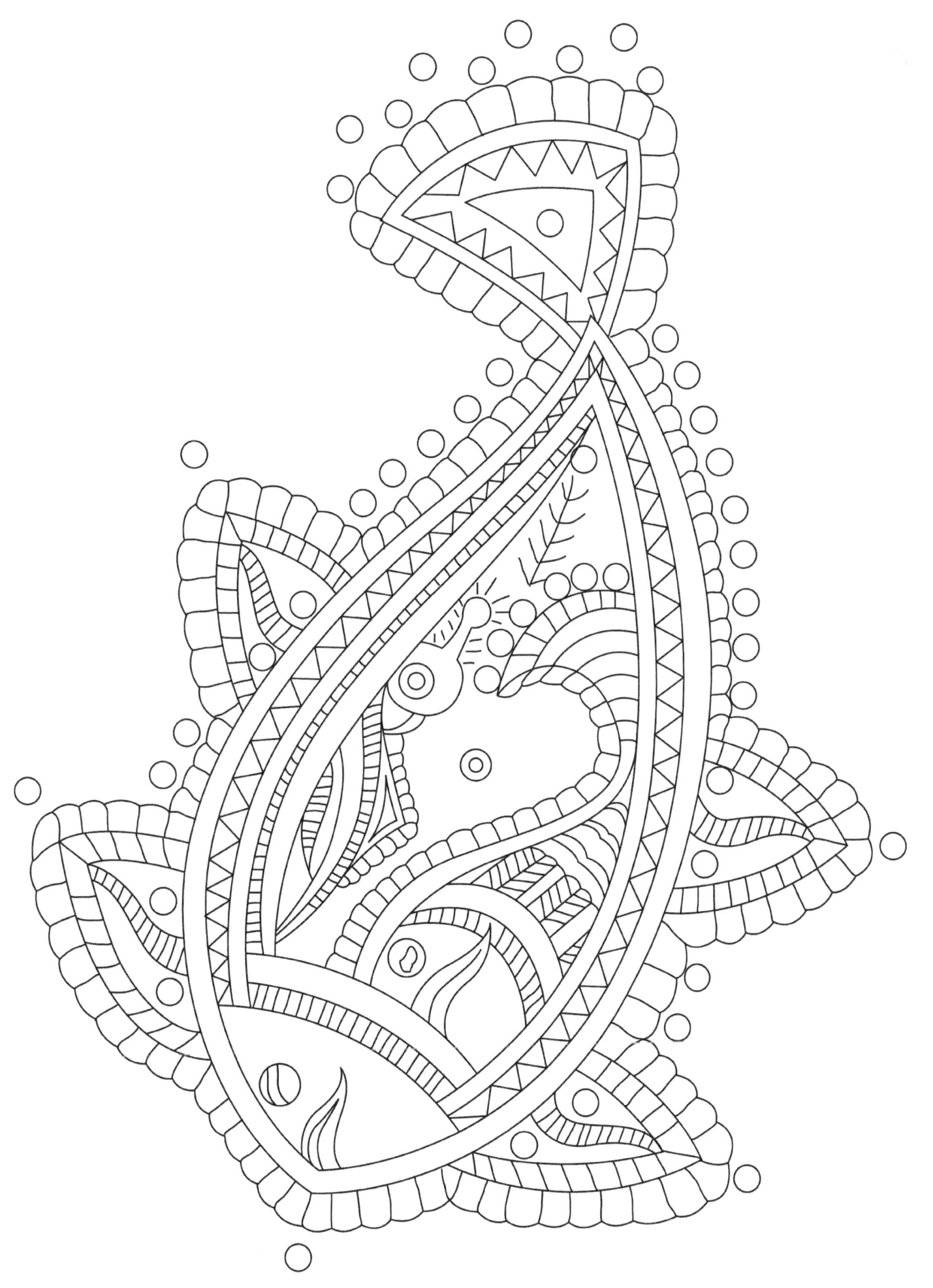

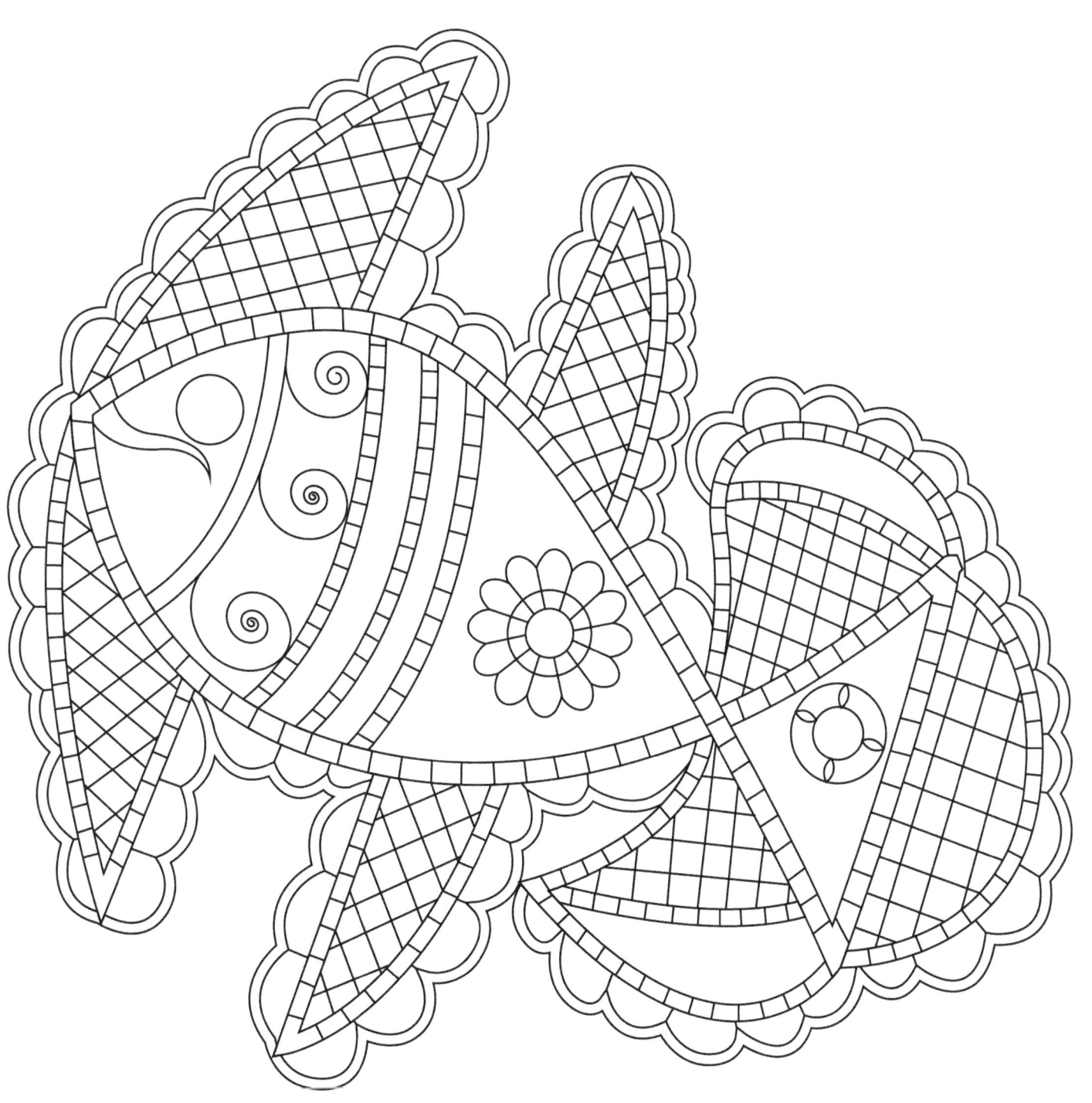

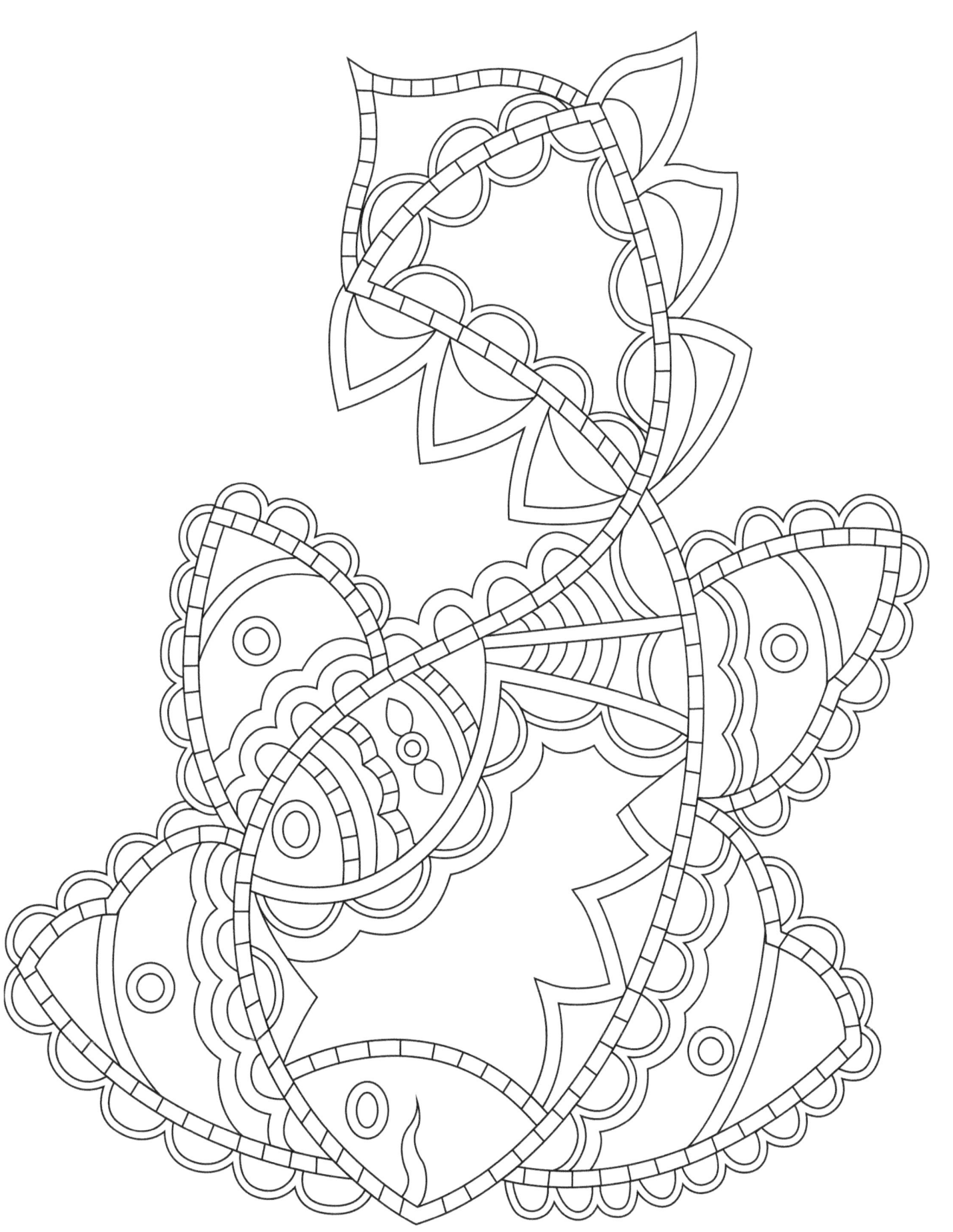

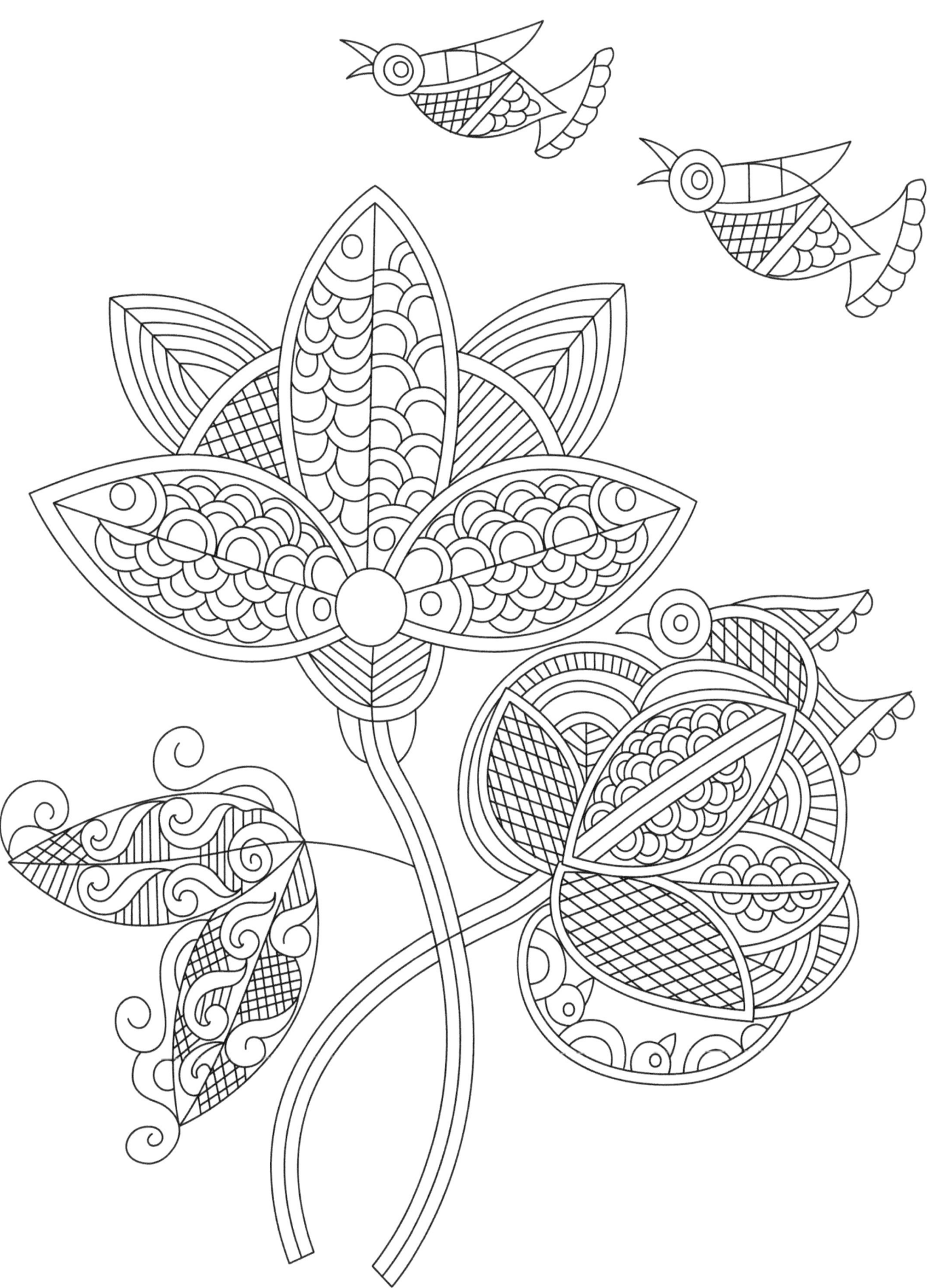

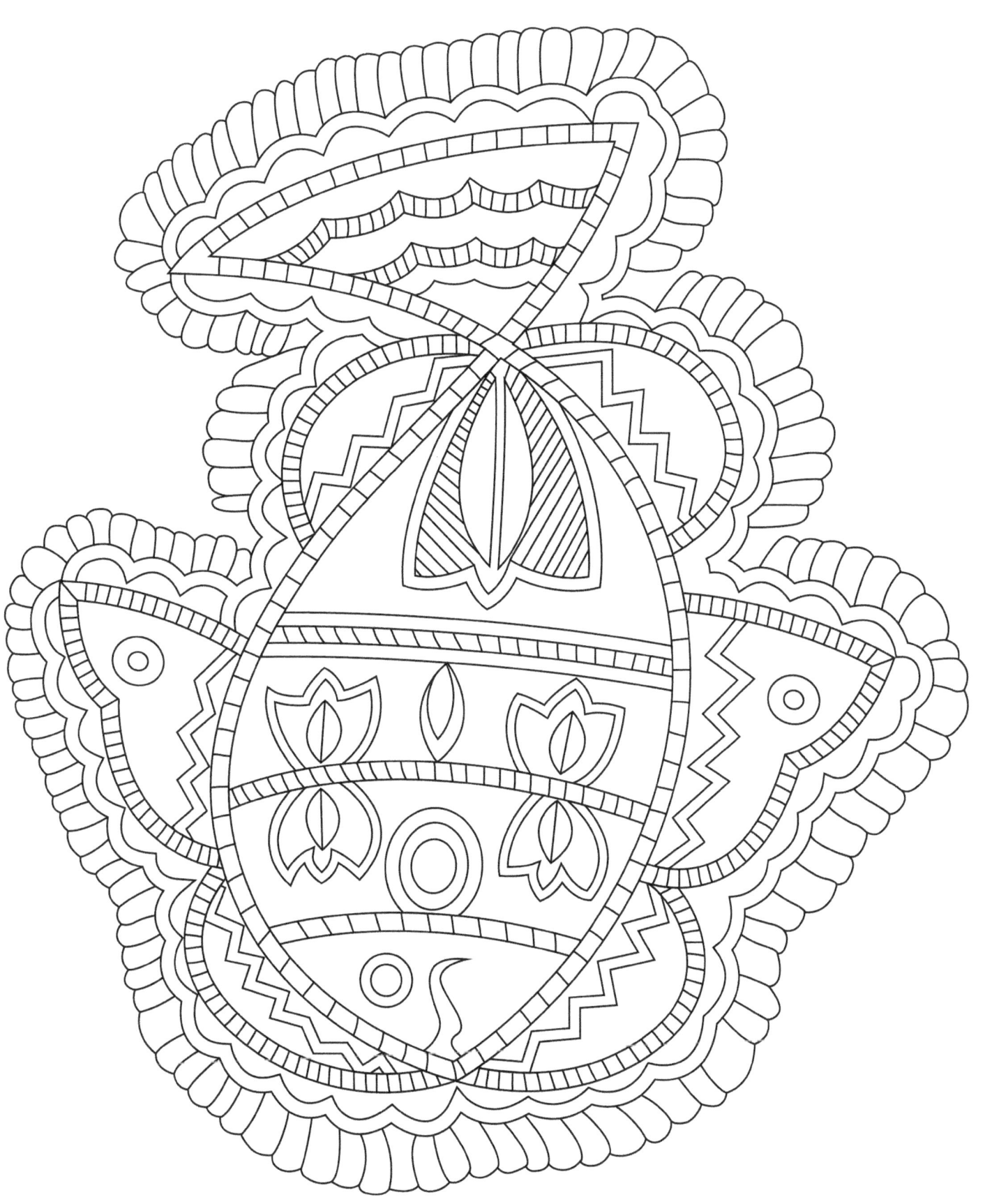

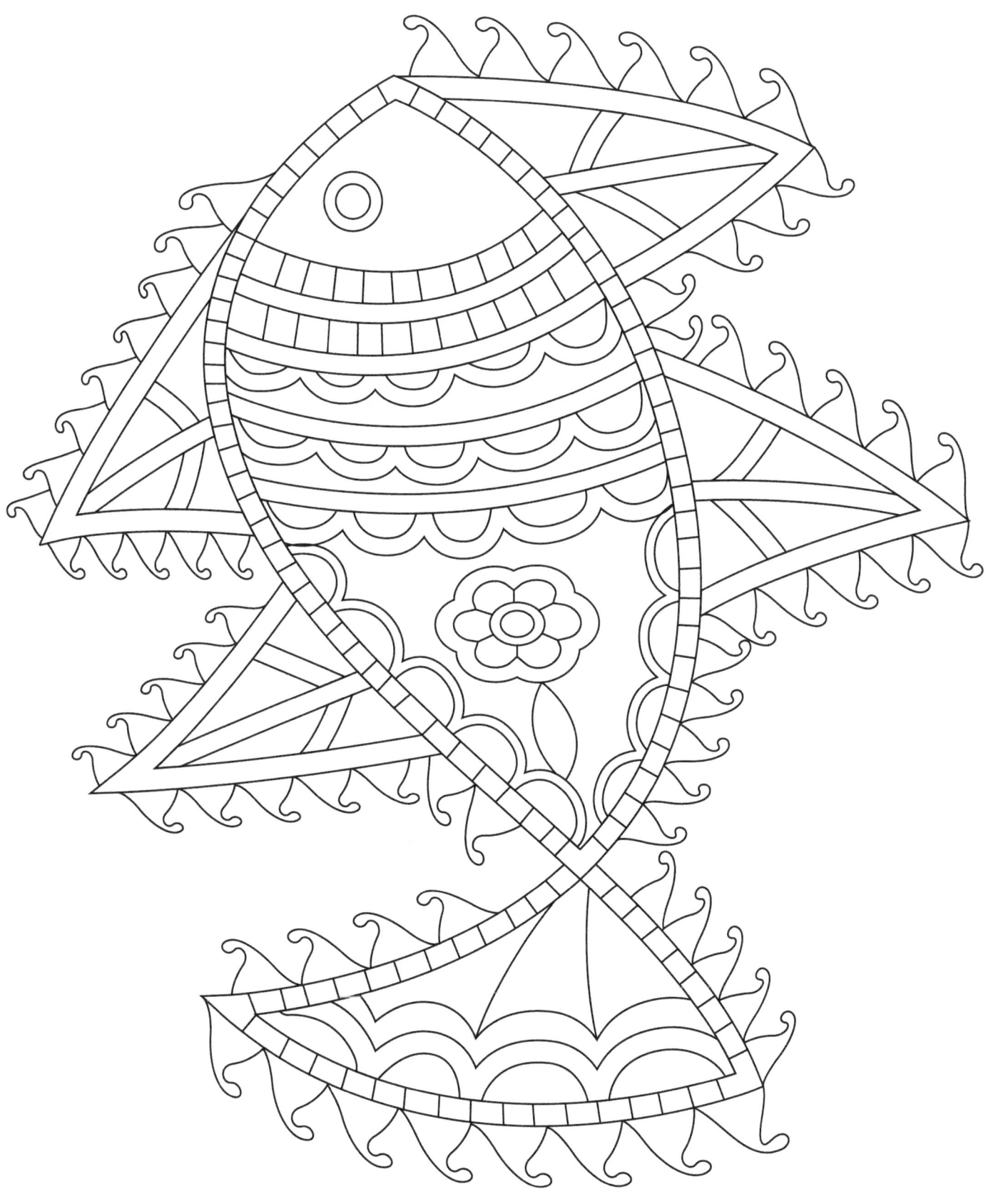

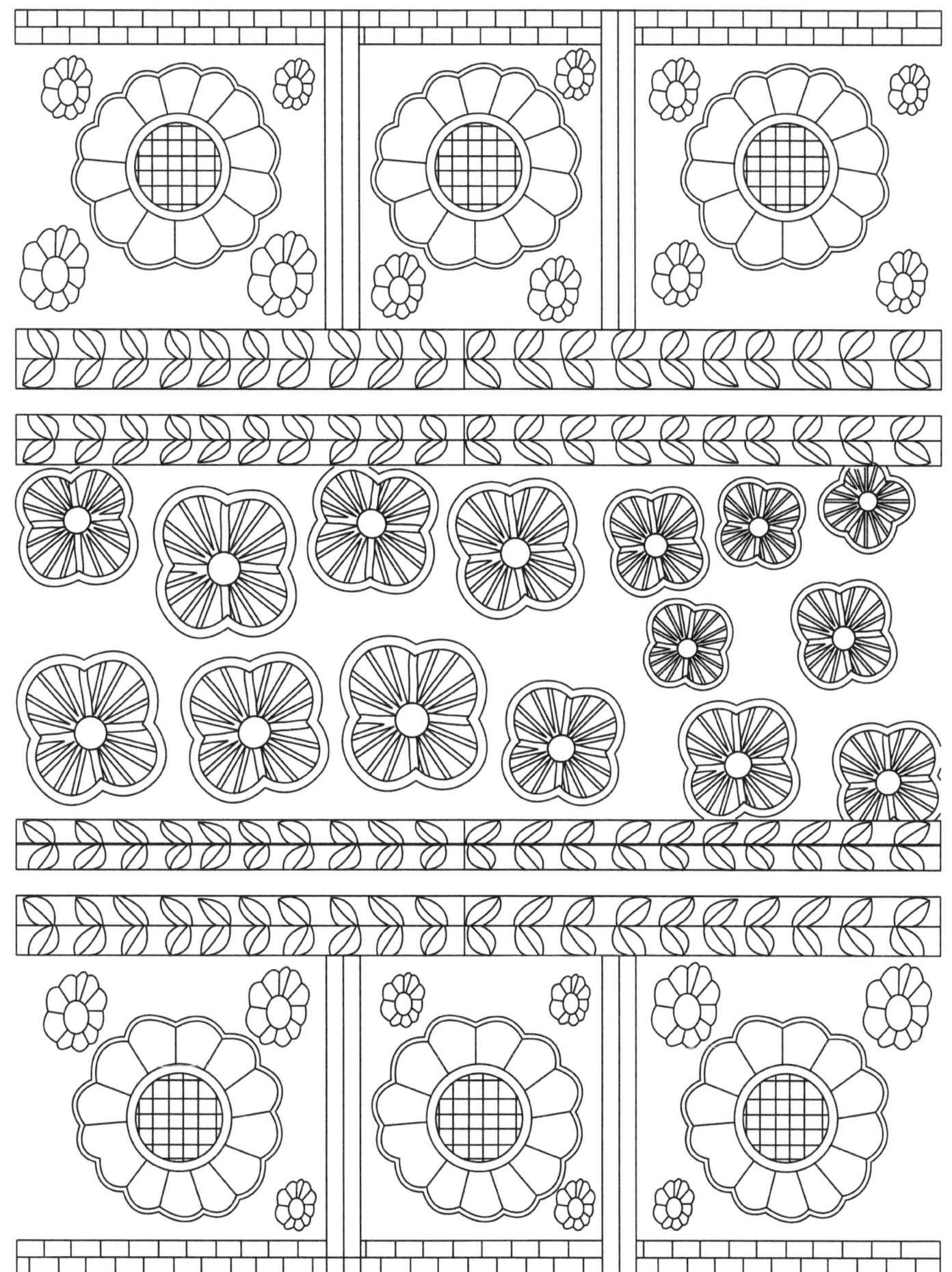

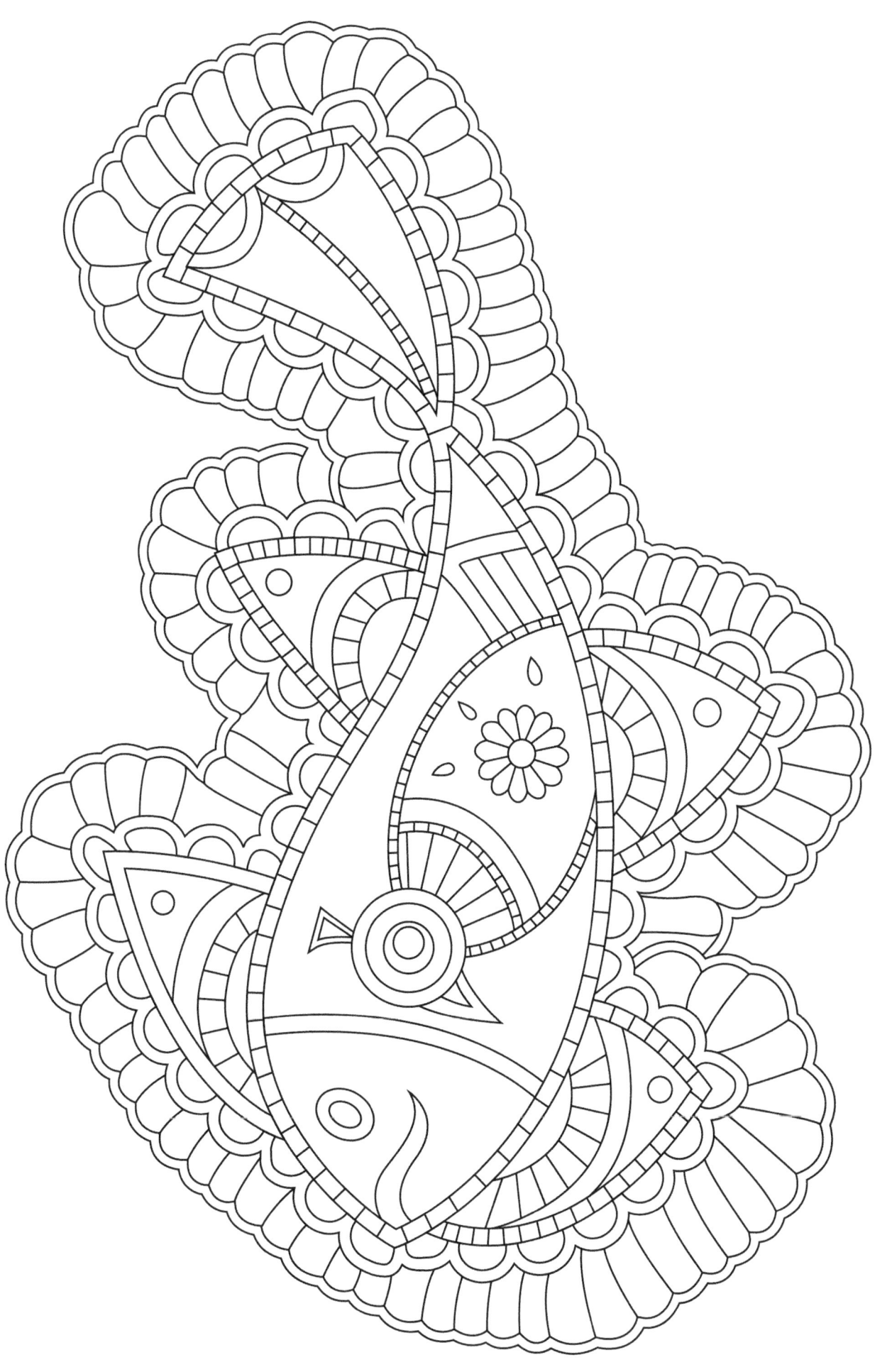

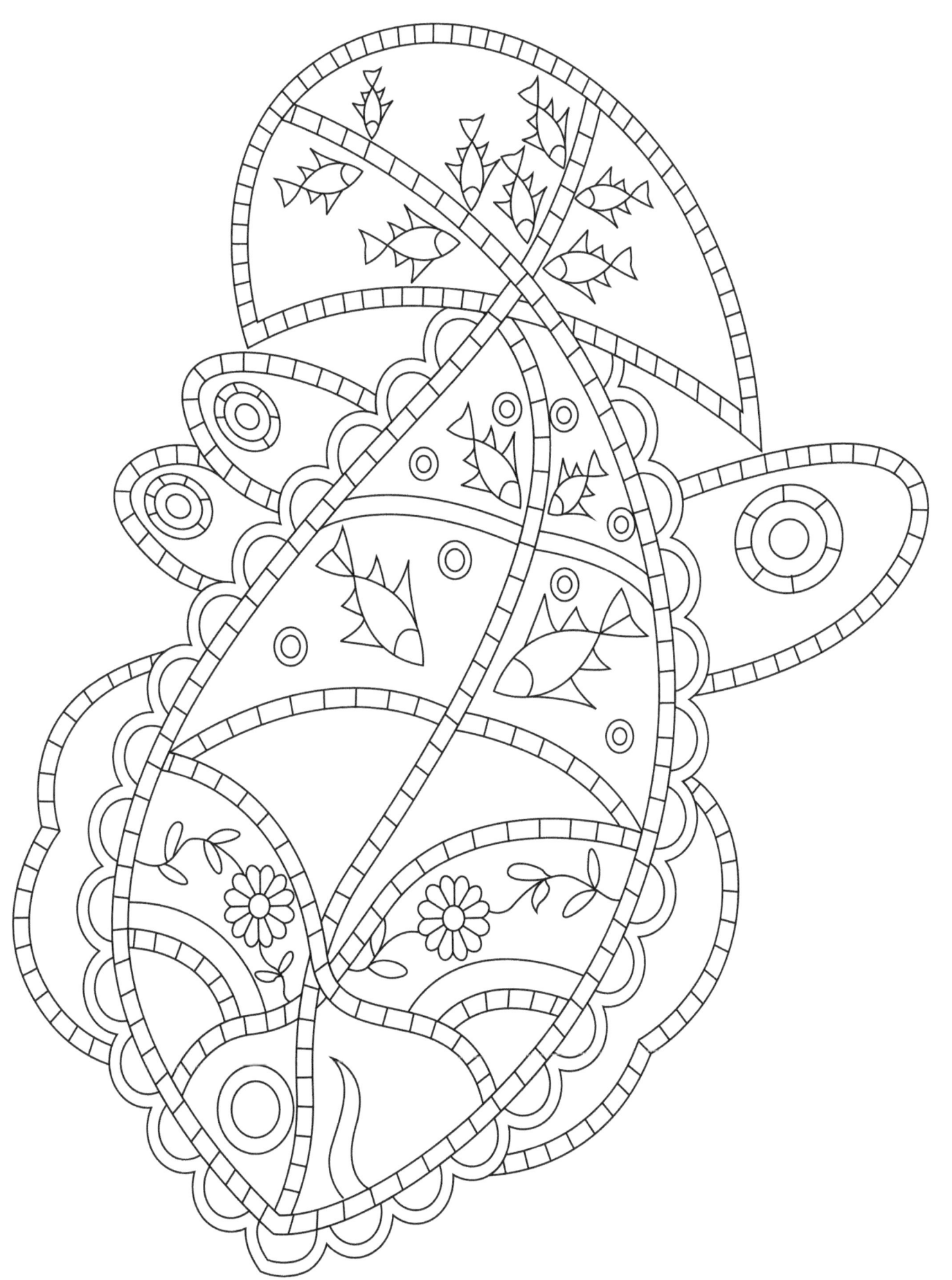

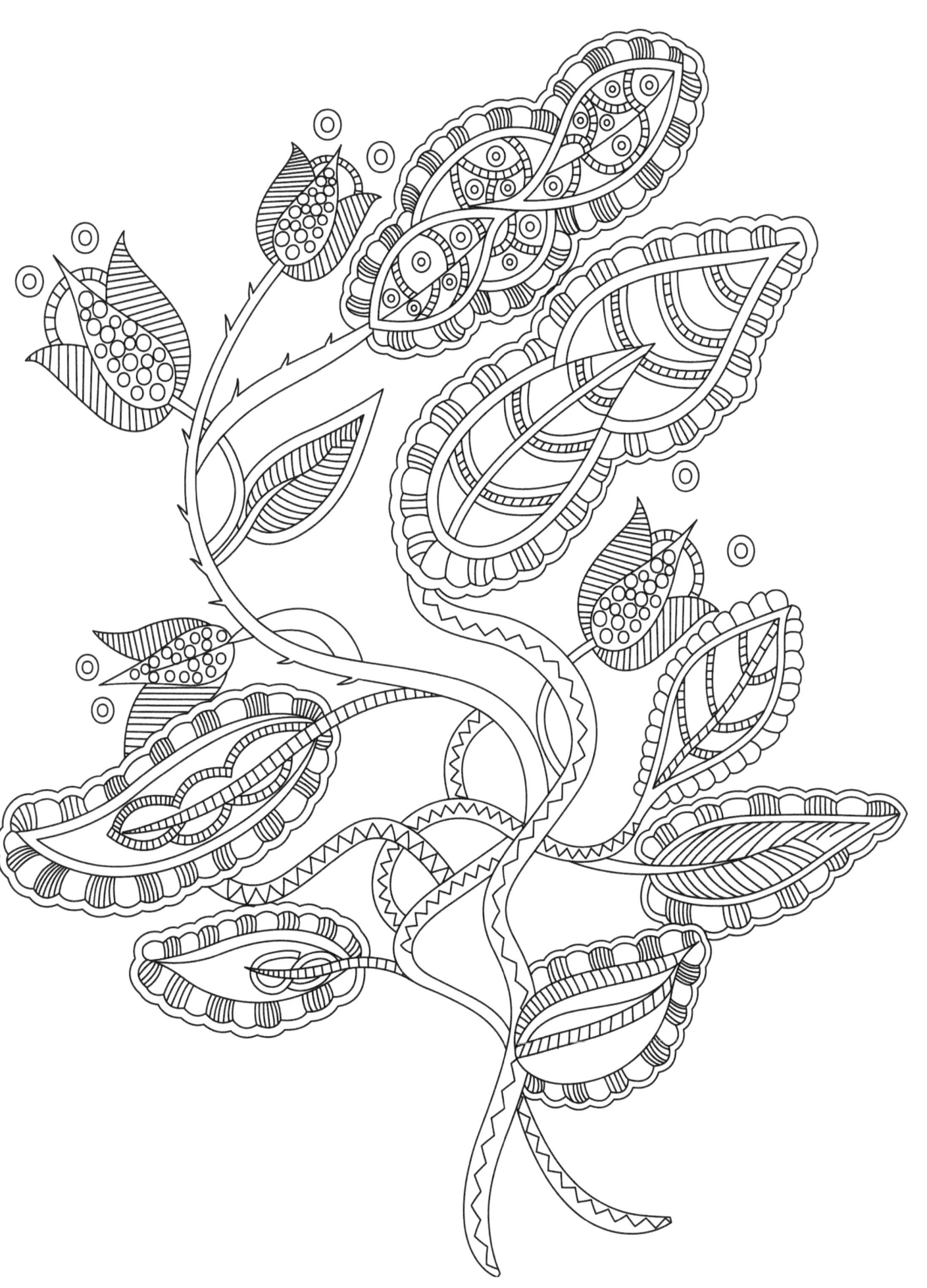

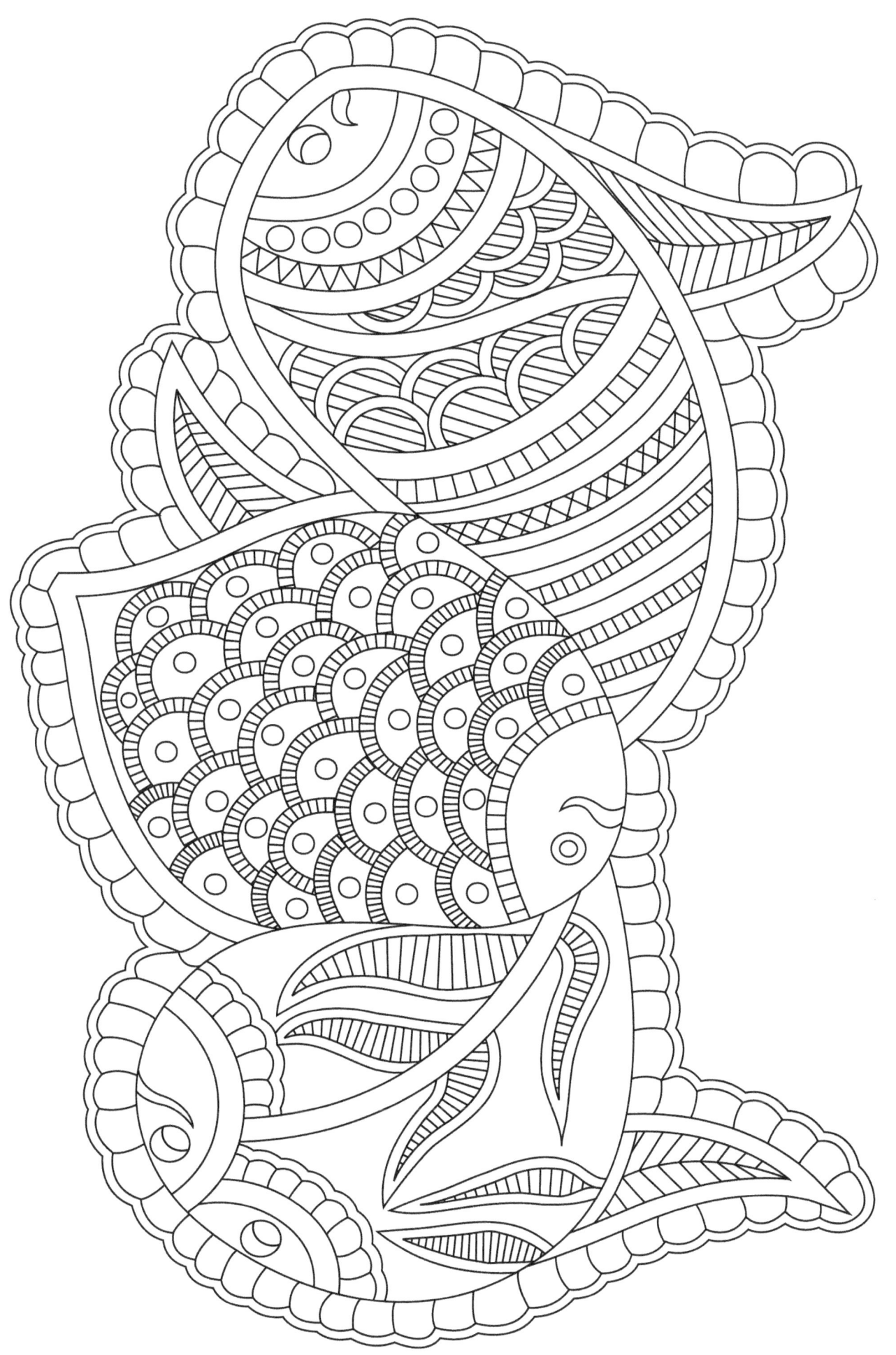

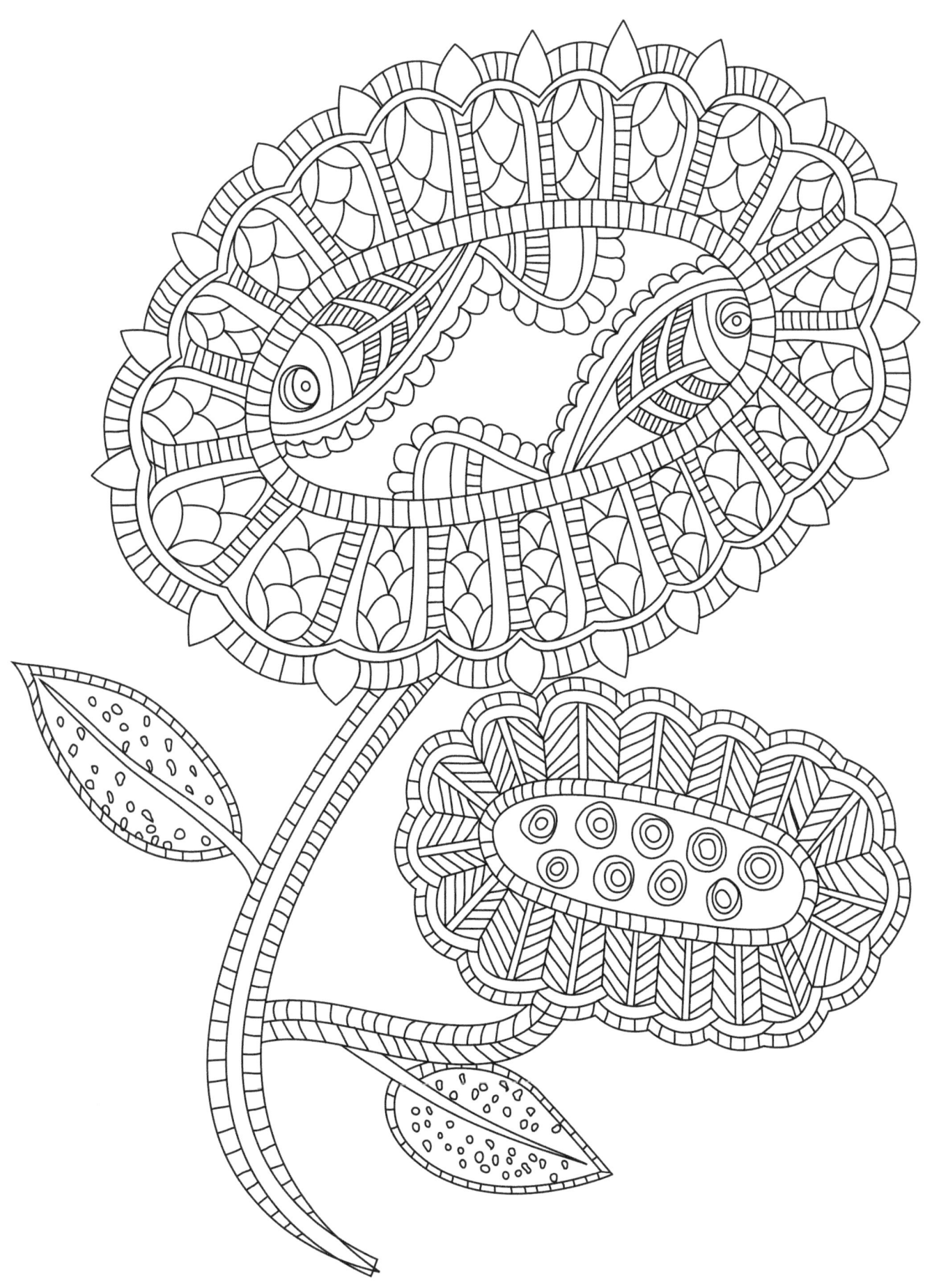

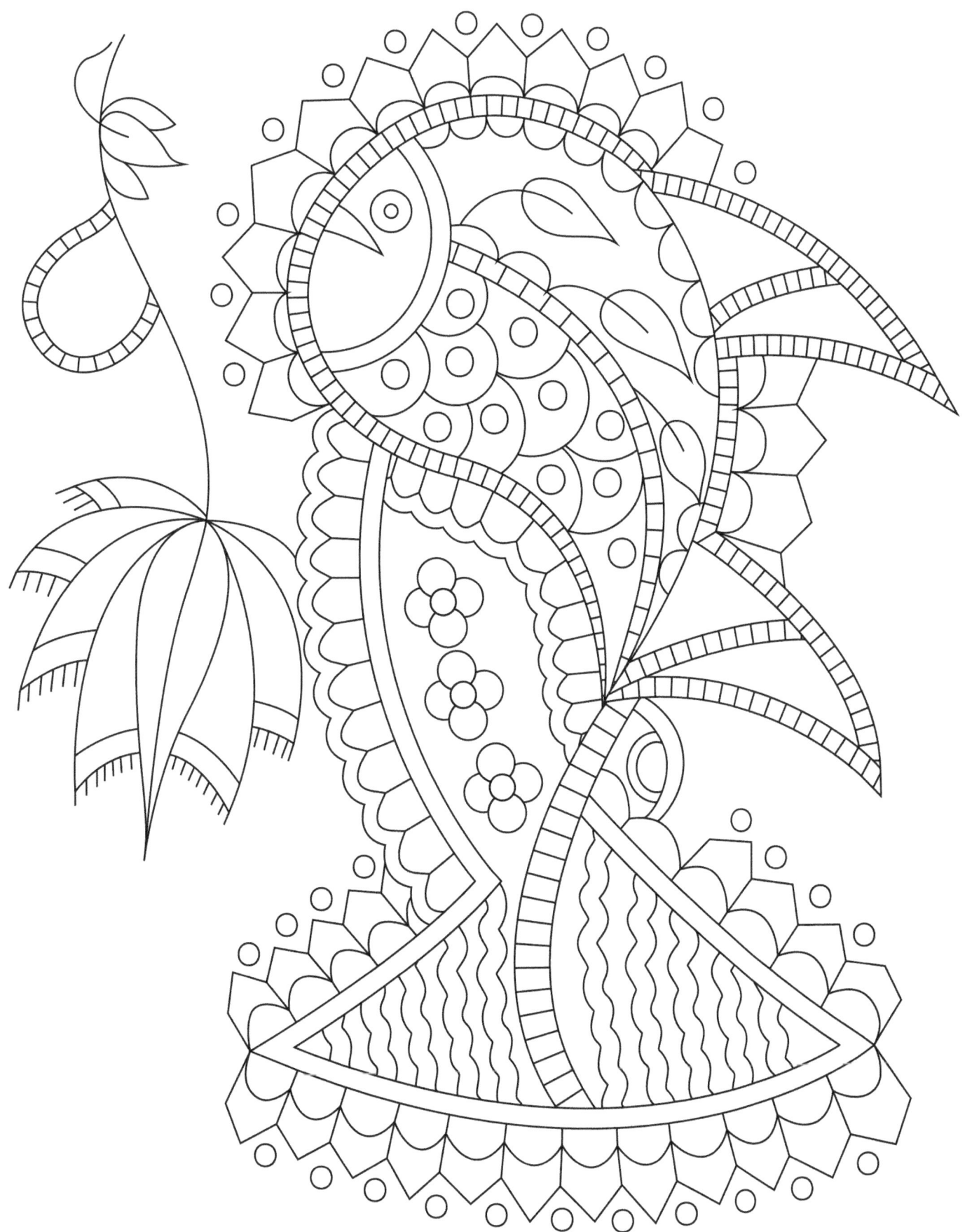

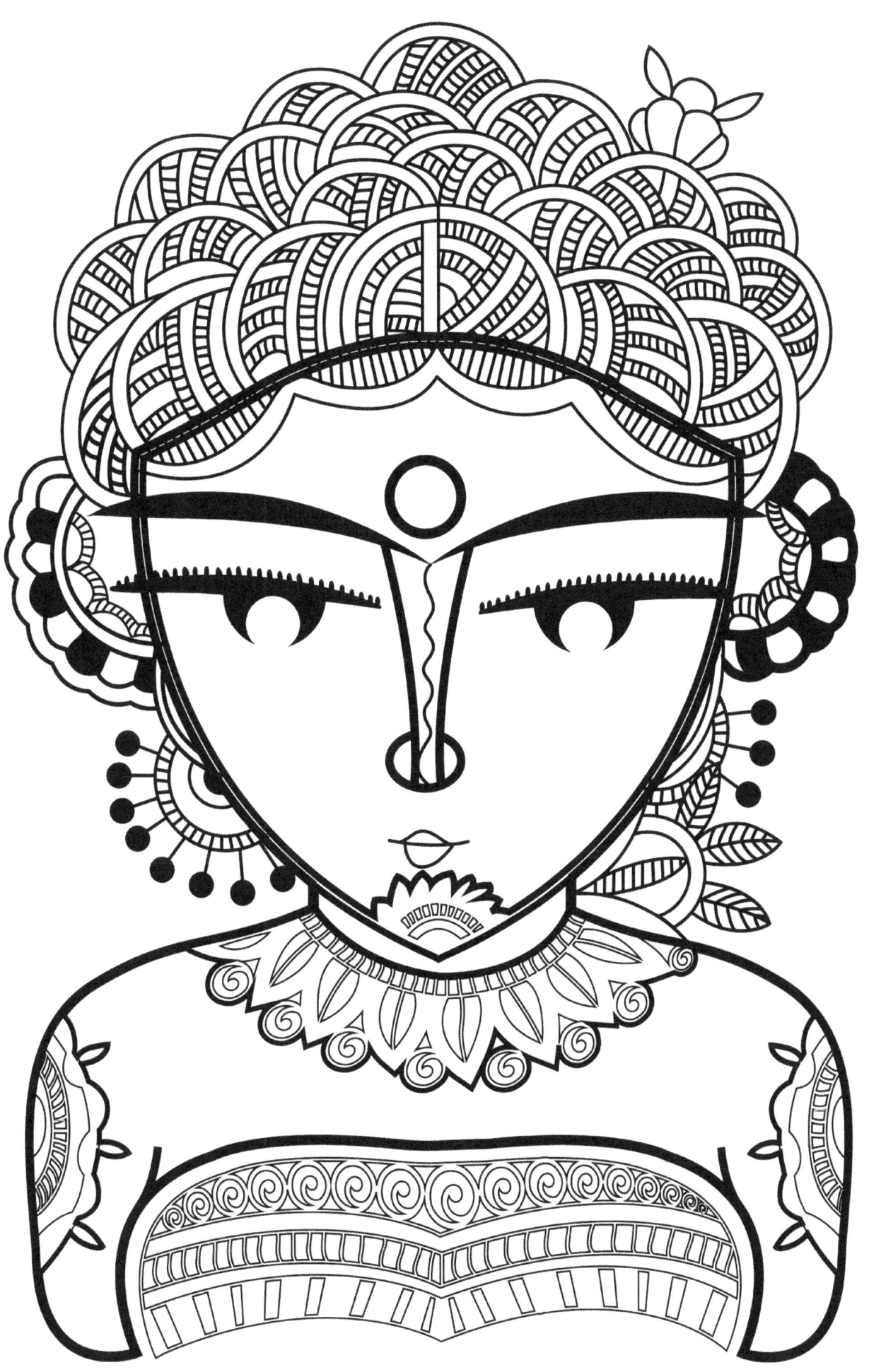

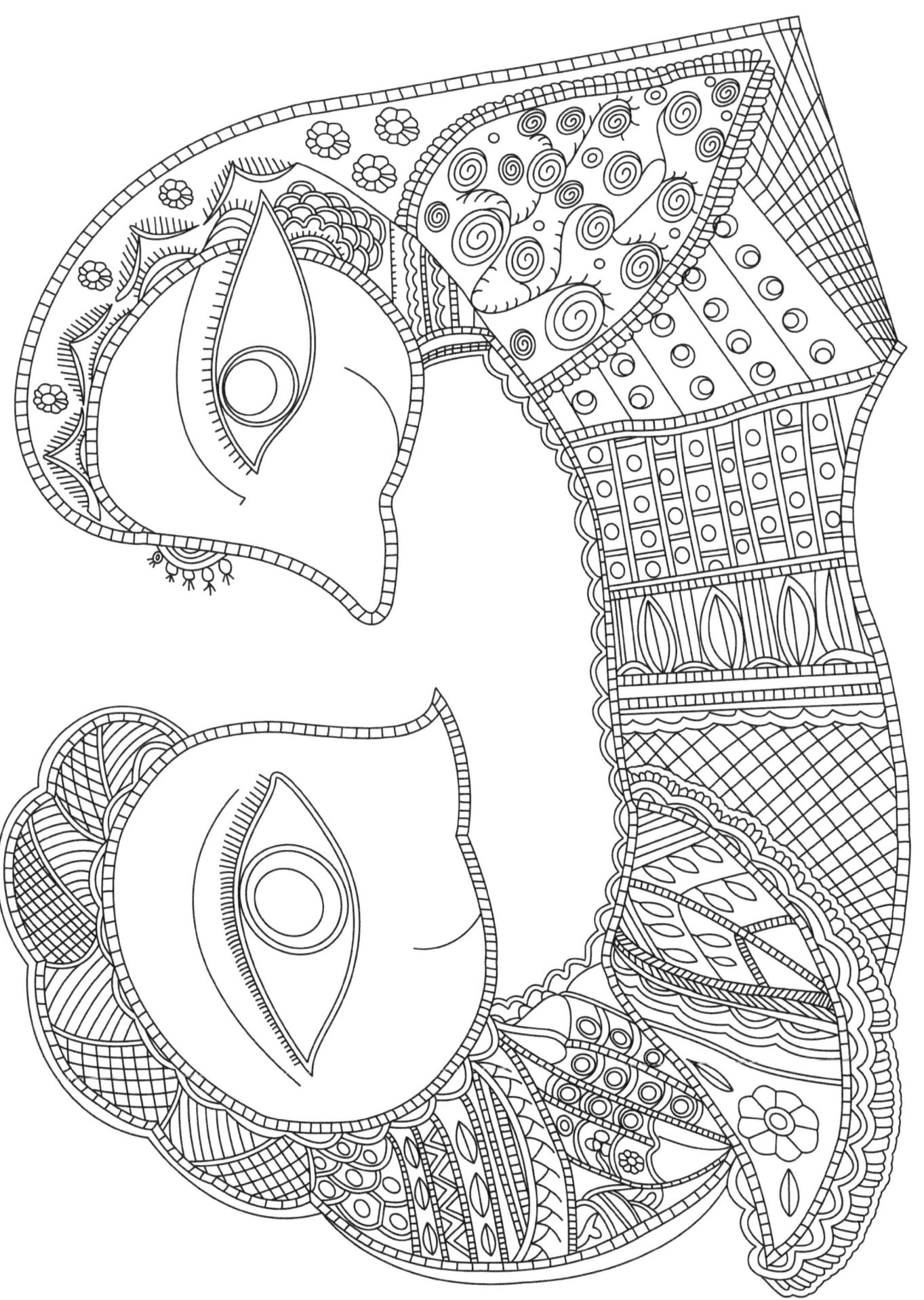

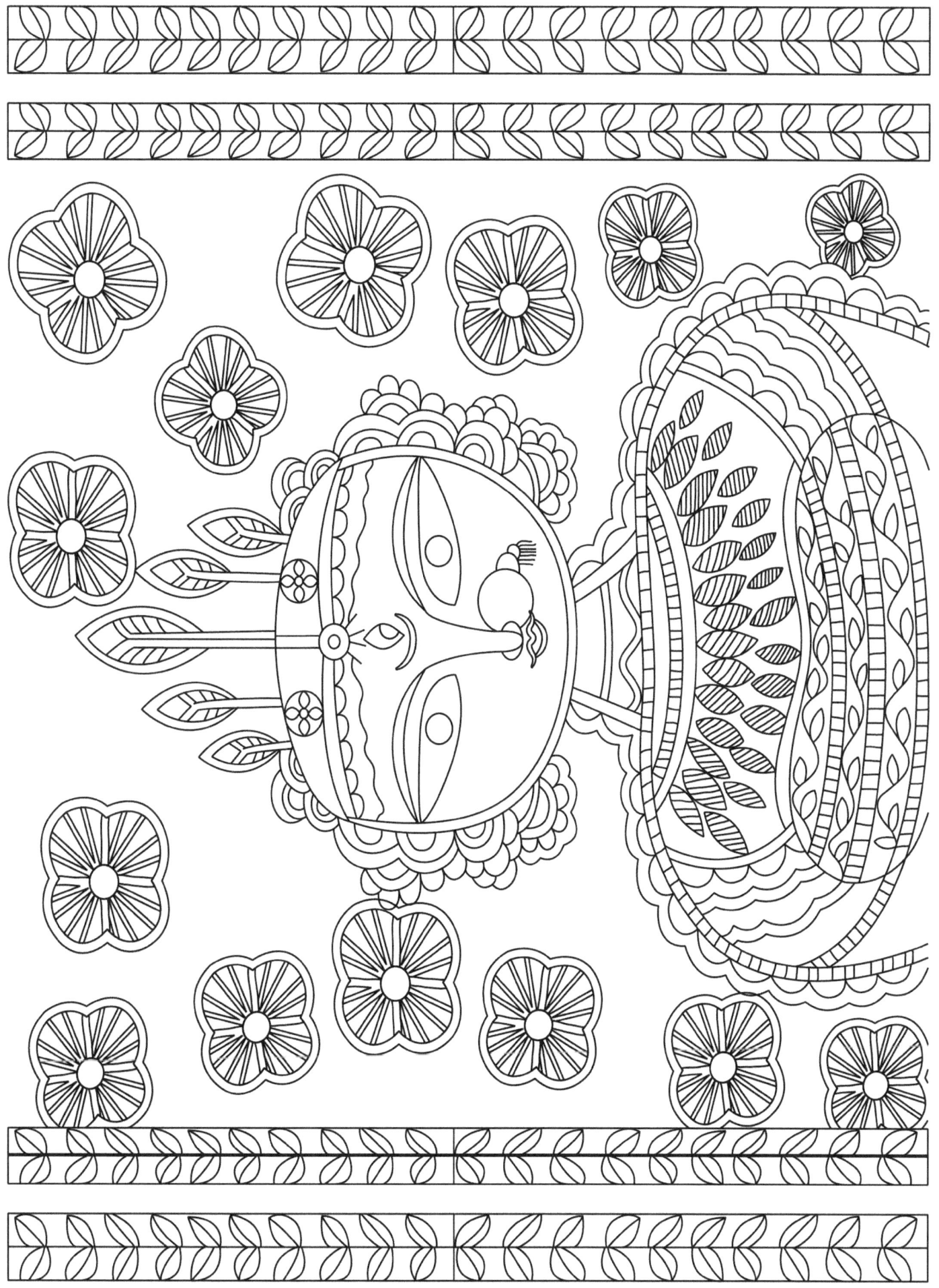

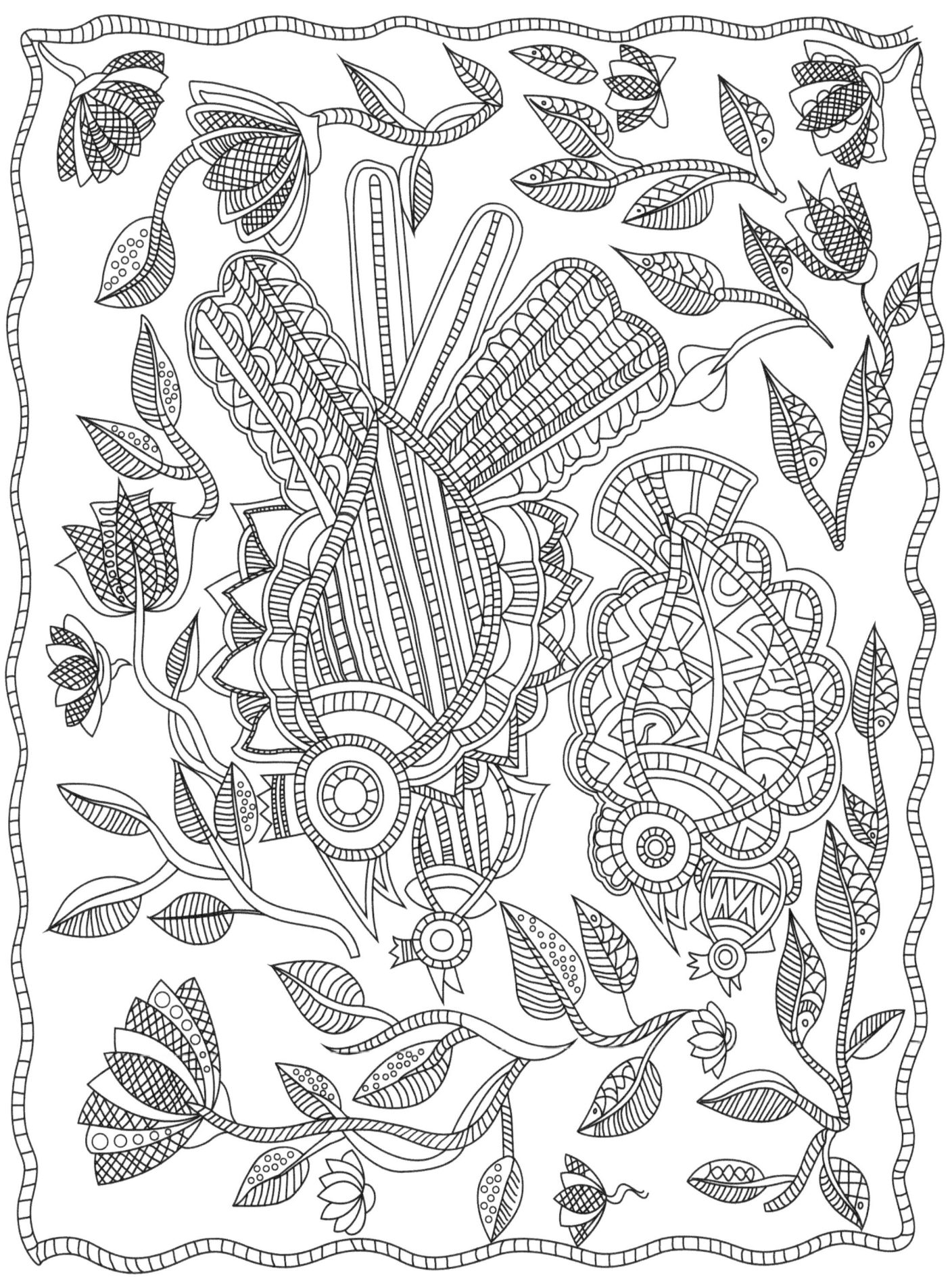

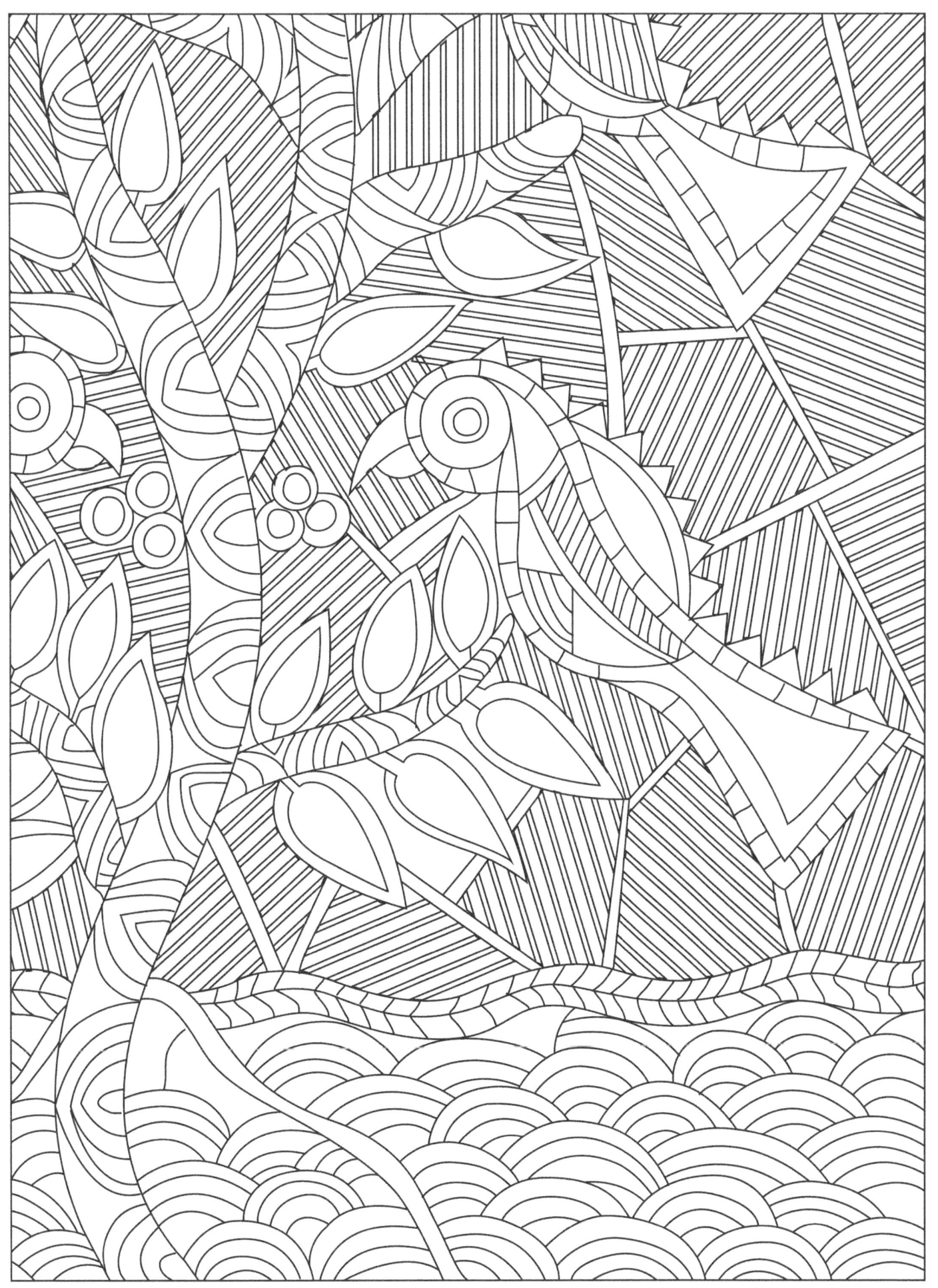

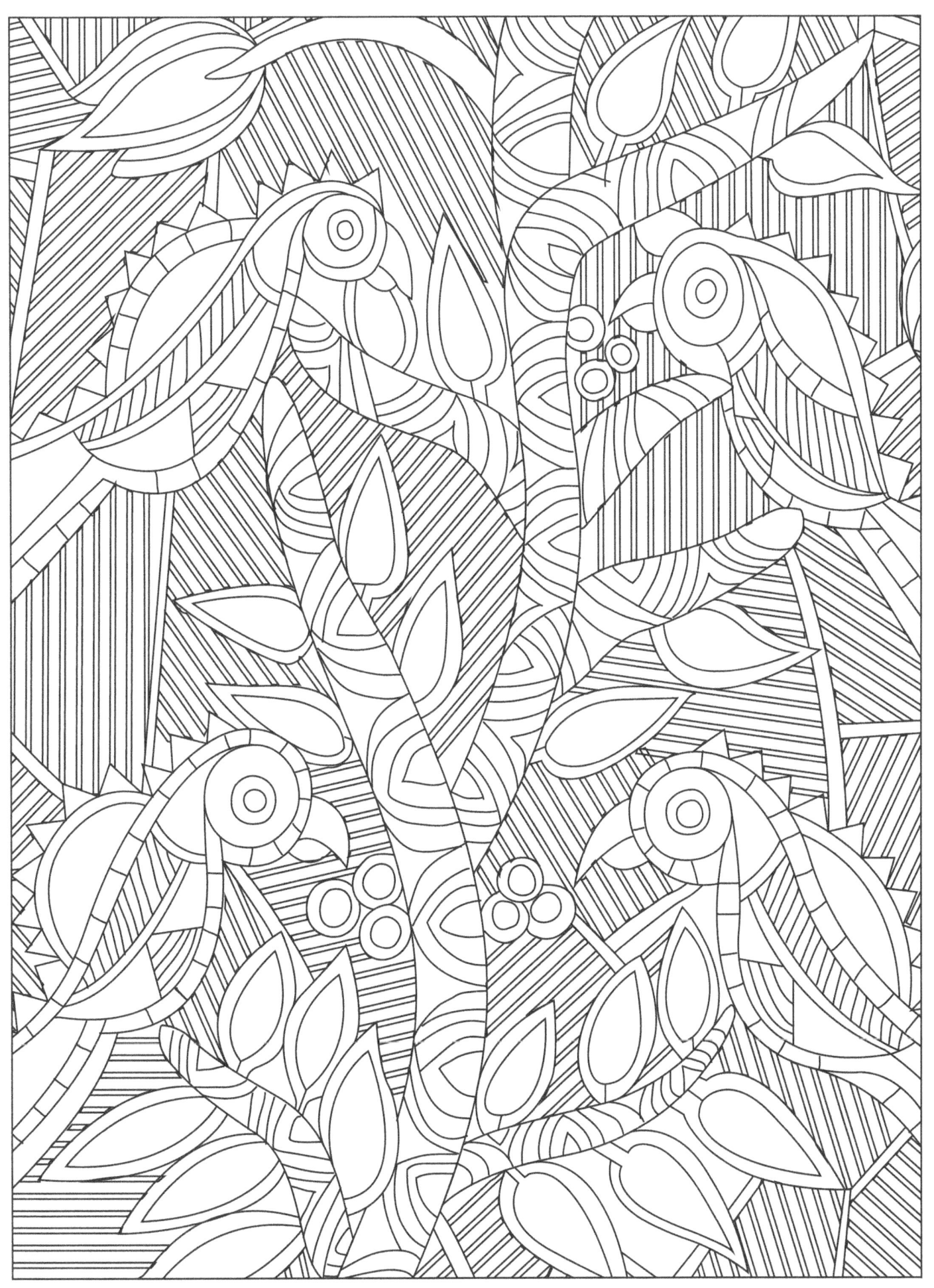

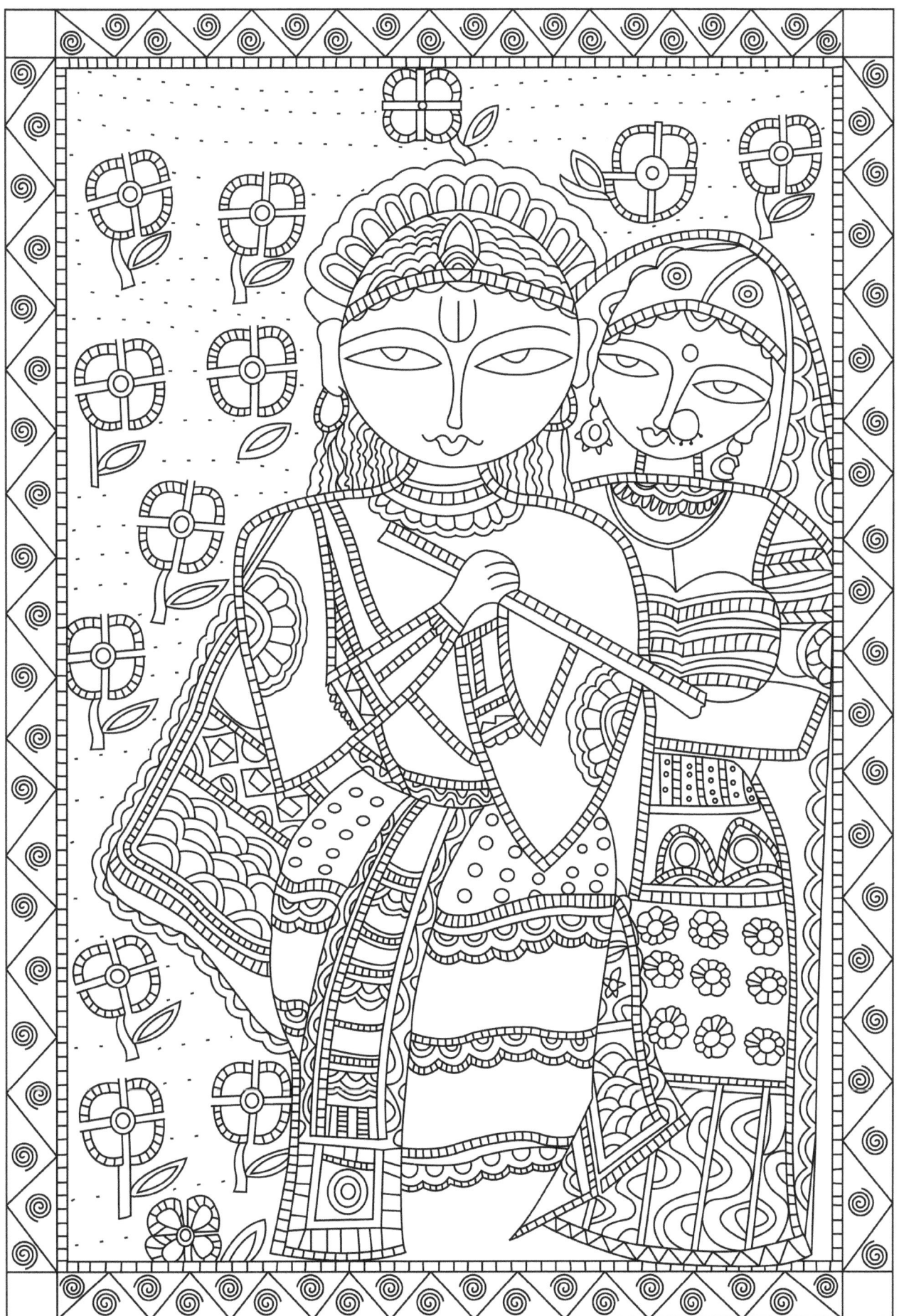

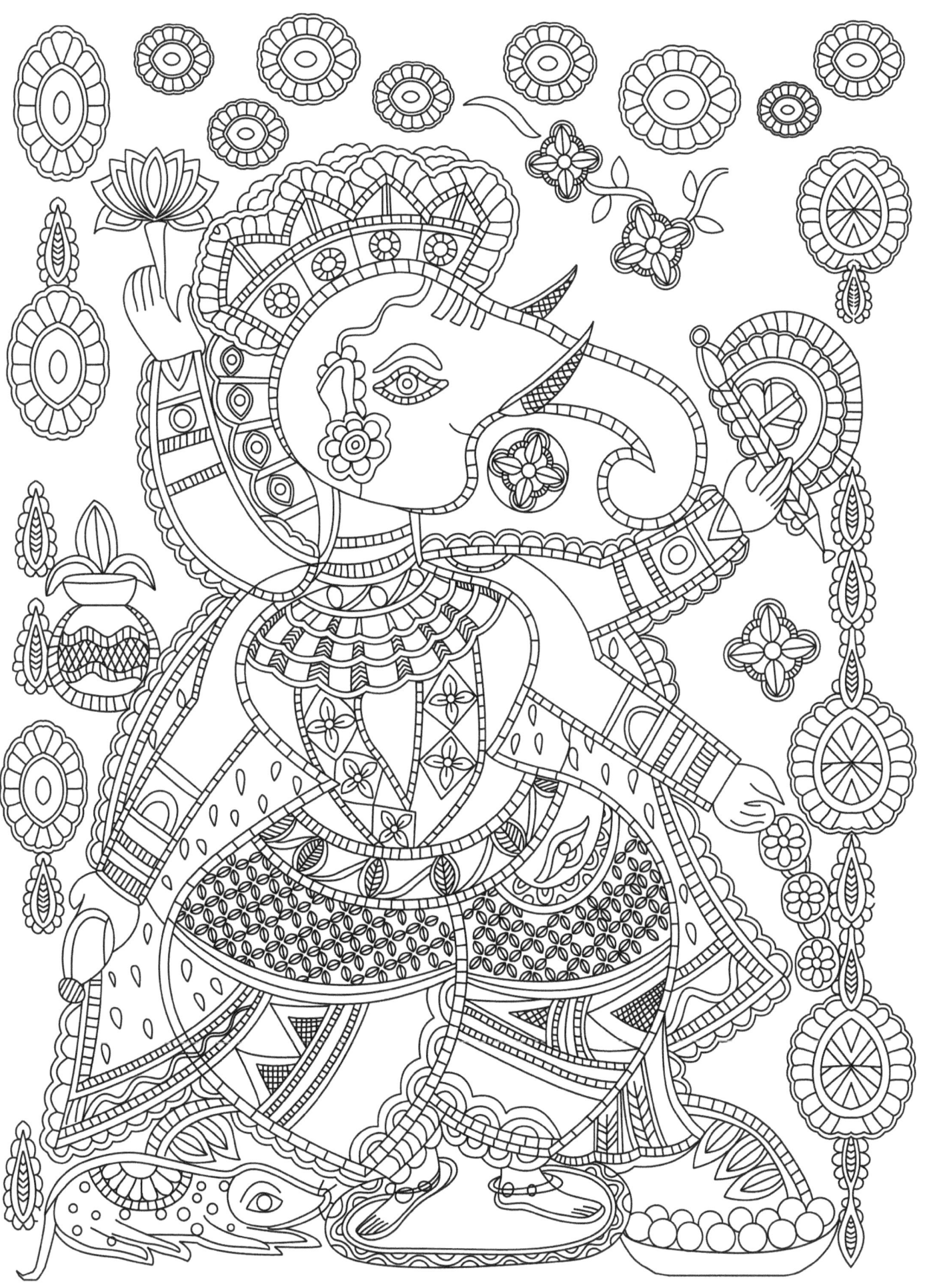

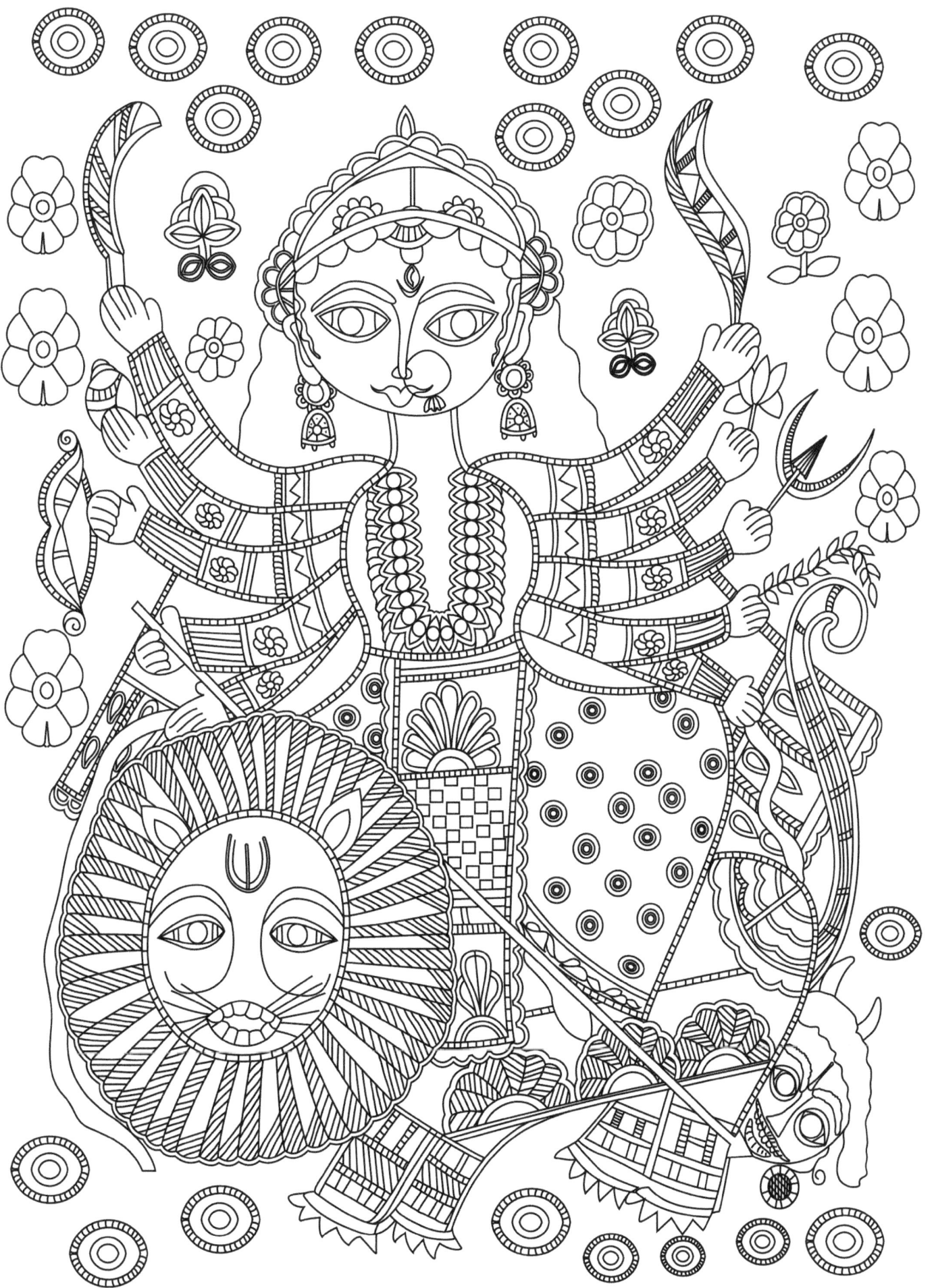

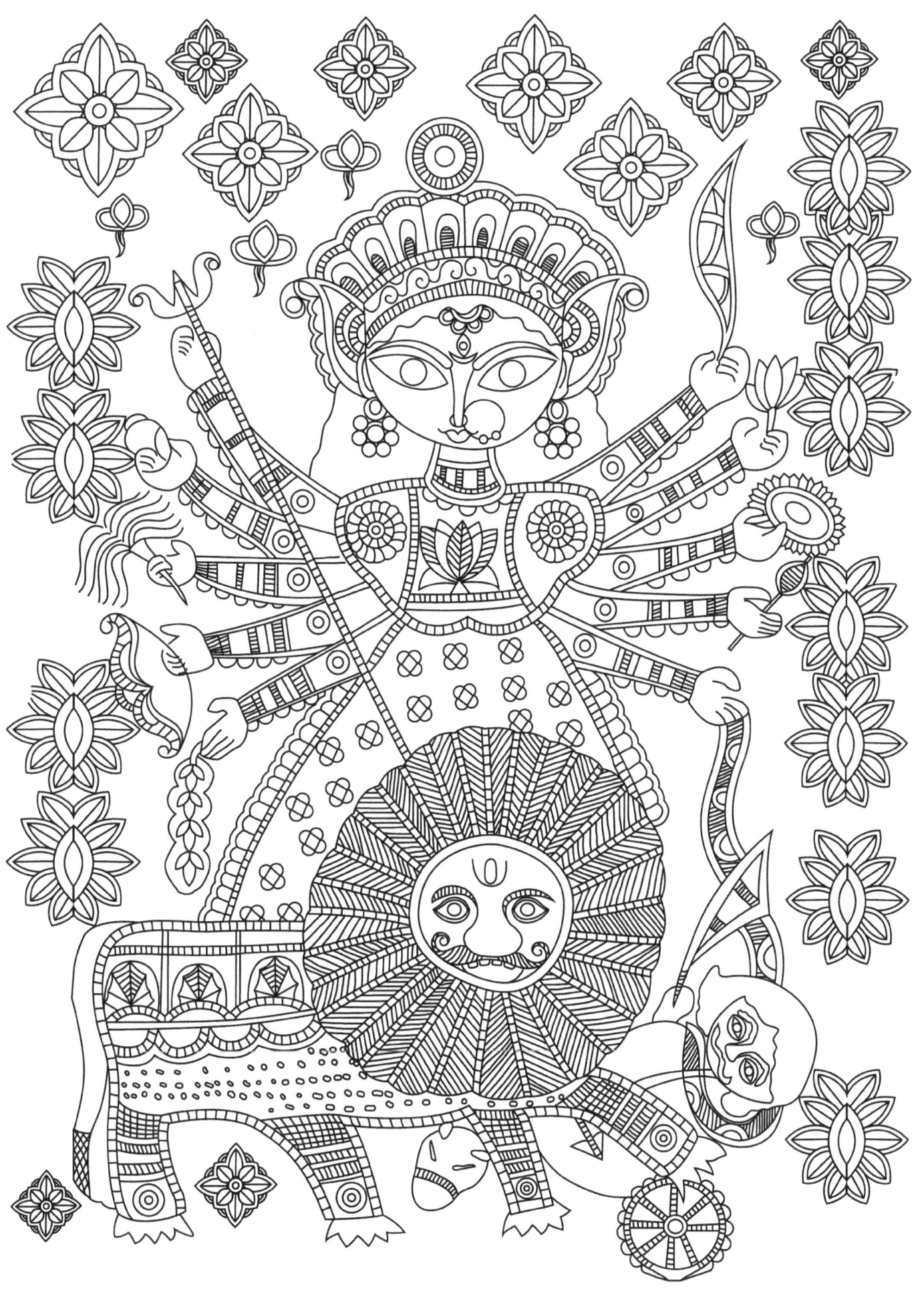

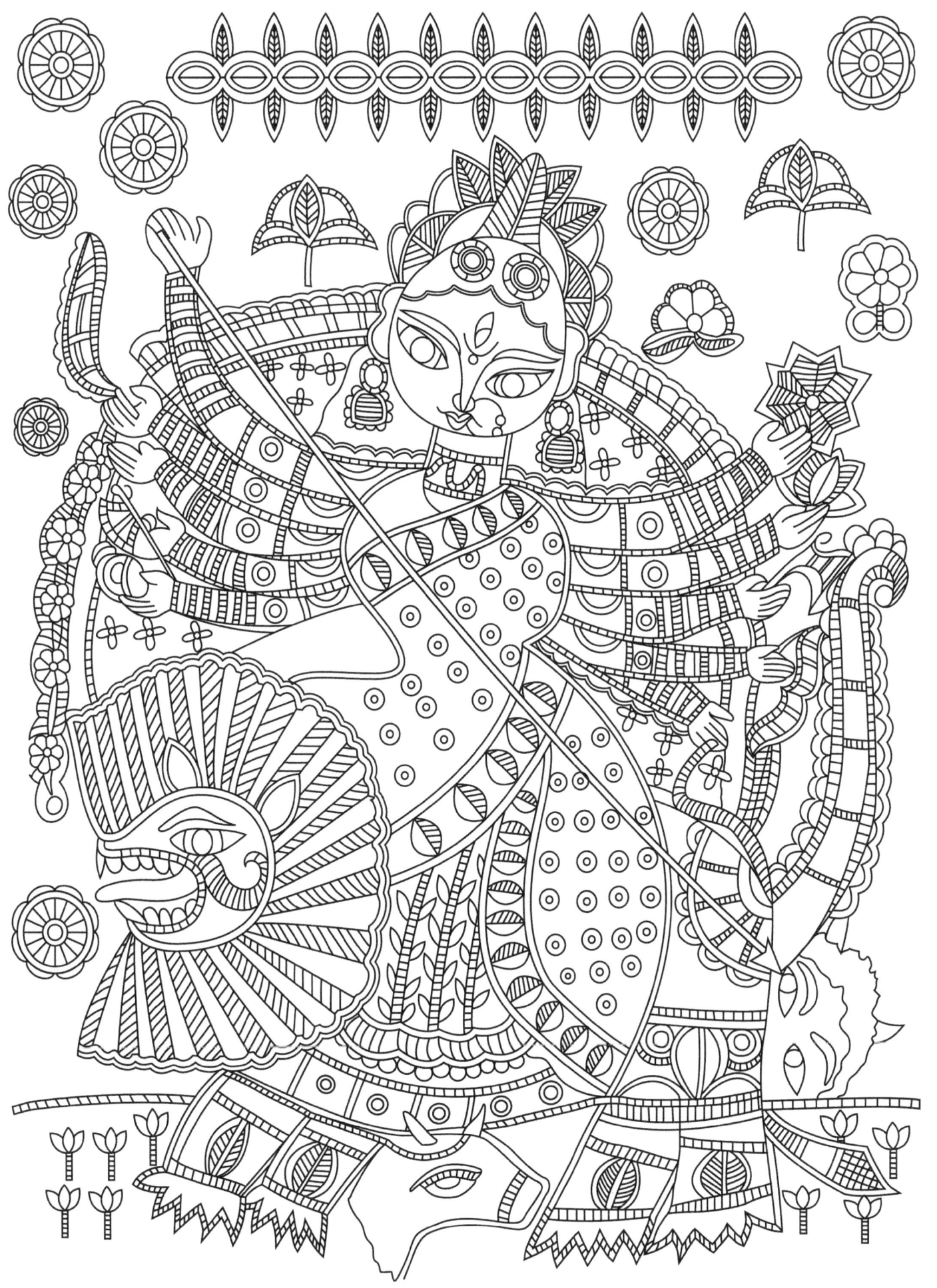

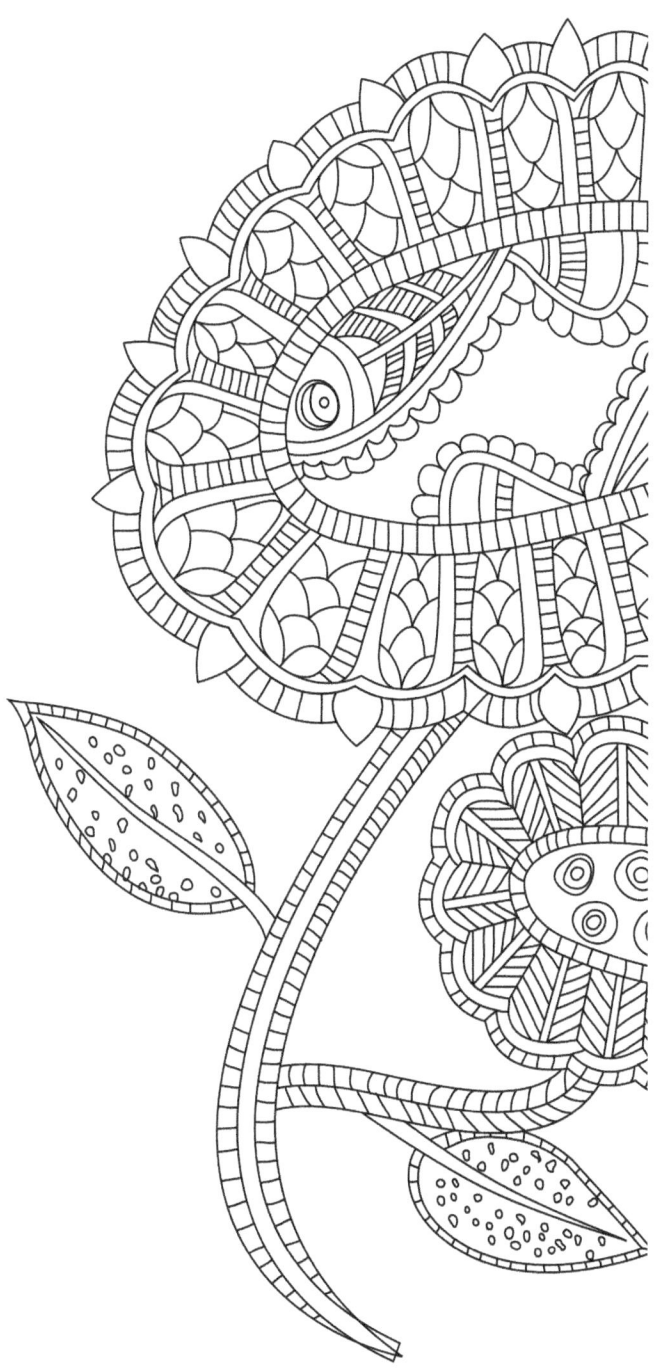

- MEET THE DESIGN TEAM -

STUDIO 324 is an art studio with 3 designers, whose creative minds work 24 hours a day.

Our illustrations are a result of the collaboration of unique artistic voices. Check out our other work on Instagram @Studio324

SHIKHA BANERJEE is a trained artist whose forte lies in exploring geometric patterns from the South-Asian region, be it the infamous spiritual symbols of Mandalas, Alpana Art from the eastern part of India, or the Madhubani forms you see in this book.

Studio 324 collaborated with Shikha Banerjee to create these digitized illustrations of original hand drawn Madhubani art pieces, to be able to bring to you our first Madhubani colouring book for adults.

Our studio loves to explore different artistic styles and we hope you love colouring what we enjoy creating!

www.ingramcontent.com/pod-product-compliance
Lightning Source LLC
Chambersburg PA
CBHW080843170526
45158CB00009B/2618